FOR WANT AND SOUND

MELISSA BUZZEO

TRENCHART: SURPLUS

♭

LES FIGUES PRESS
Los Angeles

For Want and Sound
FIRST EDITION

Text design by Emma Williams and Teresa Carmody

ISBN 13: 978-1-934254-40-0
ISBN 10: 1-934254-40-1
Library of Congress Control Number: 2012952076

Les Figues Press thanks its subscribers for their support and reader-
ship. Les Figues Press is a 501c3 organization. Donations are
tax-deductible.

Les Figues would like to acknowledge the following individuals for
their generosity: Peter Binkow and Johanna Blakley, Lauren Bon,
Chris and Diane Calkins, and Coco Owen.

Les Figues Press titles are available through:
Les Figues Press, <http://www.lesfigues.com>
Small Press Distribution, <http://www.spdbooks.org>

Special thanks to Alyssa Brillinger, Elizabeth Hall, Militza Jean-
Felix, Erin Kilduff, and Shoshana Seidman.

TrenchArt 7/5

Book 6 of 6 in the TRENCHART Surplus Series.

This project is supported in part by
a generous grant from the
National Endowment for the Arts.

ART WORKS.
arts.gov

LES FIGUES PRESS

Post Office Box 7736
Los Angeles, CA 90007
info@lesfigues.com
www.lesfigues.com

For my mother, Christine.

CONTENTS

INTRODUCTION:

SENTENCE || BODY || LAW

by Rob Halpern

> *And what did you give me at birth,*
> *what did you give me at sentence.*
> Melissa Buzzeo

For Gertrude Stein, there is no greater pleasure than that of diagramming sentences. "I suppose other things may be more exciting to others when they are at school," she writes, "but to me undoubtedly when I was at school the really completely exciting thing was diagramming sentences and that has been to me ever since the one thing that has been completely exciting and completing. I like the feeling the everlasting feeling of sentences as they diagram themselves. In that way one is completely possessing something and incidentally one's self" (126).

Diagramming sentences, Stein feels a transposition of agency, an inversion of force, because the sentence is always already diagramming itself, quietly from the inside, as if the artifice of its clarity were but the effect of a structure otherwise resistant to communication. And rather than the agent of the diagram, one becomes its patient.

In other words, to be "completely possessing" one's self as a speaking subject one first has to feel oneself completely possessed *occupied, haunted* by the orders of the sentence. Only then might one break the spell of that possession, and disabuse the sentence of its delusion of mastery, which hangs on dual institutional obscurities: grammar & law. Melissa Buzzeo's *For Want and Sound* registers the pulse of Stein's revelation: the sentence, however fragmented and inoperative, bears the impress of the forces that produce it *linguistic force, social force* even as these forces remain below the threshold of articulation.

Stein discovers the self as an incident of the sentence, an obscure moment of the diagram: the self as mere accident of grammar, by-product of whatever conventions govern the relations between subjects & objects. Under the lawful spell of grammar, one finds one's self a sentenced thing. The pleasure *completely exciting* of diagramming sentences thus becomes the pleasure of undoing, suspending one's self-possession in the fault between body and law, the pleasure *completely possessing* of one's own suspension.

Like the speaking subjects of Buzzeo's writing, I am aroused in the process of grasping this as I fantasize some relief from the real illusions of custom & costume.

•

Whereas Buzzeo's preceding book, *Face*, is inspired by recognition and presence, the book that you are holding now is informed by apocalypse, devastation and wreck: "some document ledger buried in the ground to survive destruction" ("An Elegy For Passage: For Want and Sound" 22). *For Want and Sound* is haunted by disaster, this undoing of the stars, a fatelessness defying prediction and predication alike: the incommensurability of a coming otherness (outside) that's always already cohabitating with the present (inside), an incommensurability whose pressure on grammar and syntax is a pressure our sentences often can't bear, despite how hard they try, especially when the subjects of those sentences have been undone *dispossessed* by the losses they attempt to narrate. "You give up so much face force and are surprised to feel nothing," Buzzeo writes, and *For Want and Sound* becomes the structure of that feeling (100).

This may be Stein's everlasting feeling: the ecstasy of suspension whereby the finitude of the sentence comes undone. *For Want and Sound* opens on the space of this suspension, a blank where the body never stops coming.

As Judith Butler reminds us, when one becomes ek-static, beside oneself in rage or grief or pleasure, "transported beyond oneself by a passion," one's sentences can only falter (24). In other words, when one is ecstatic one cannot be sovereign as one's sentences stumble or break.

This is a book about the body and the sentence, at once grammatical and juridical. It concerns language and law, force and longing, and the fate of love that can't be contained by our sentences, there being no socially sanctioned form for that excess. How is one to communicate a sentence whose subject wants more than grammar allows? And what might this want sound like?

•

The sound will never coincide with its document.

The document will never coincide with its testimony.

The testimony will never coincide with its subject.

The subject will never coincide with its body.

The body will never coincide with its longing.

The longing will never coincide with its sentence.

The sentence will never coincide with its law.

The law will never coincide with its sound.

The sound will never coincide with its articulation.

•

Separateness arises from identifying the self with the body.
                    Brihadaranayaka Upanishad

A sound enters language in a state of separation: alienation from its source (distress). A sentence can't narrate the forces that make it. *For Want and Sound* constructs a narrative whose sounds and sentences derive from documents and testimonies with which they will never adequately correspond.[1] The writing moves toward this impossible story while drowning in the sound of another.[2] Neither can be recovered *from*

---

1. "In the 1980s and into the beginning of the next decade a series of ritual abuse cases were tried all over the country in the American suburbs. Preschool teachers day care workers teachers at the public schools often young often queer often poor always naked in some marked cultural way were accused of ritualistic repeated assault. Sexual assault of the most fantastical kind of rings of children. Hidden doors traps doors costumes. Red lips and desire. […] There are records twenty years later that sometimes the police visited a single child's house eighty times and hypnotized them eighty times reading a script of another child's abuse before getting a testimony and giving the child relief and often a badge. Language doesn't come from nothing." Buzzeo, "An Elegy" (13-14).

2. "The body of water surrounding Long Island and separating it on one side from the states of Connecticut and Rhode Island. Once heavily populated by Native Americans this peninsula culture formed by glacial moraine was colonized early by the Dutch and then the British and

violence, from flood, from contamination in sentences that can only fail to cover the bodies left in their wake. Two books.[3] Sound escapes, sentences remain: and in the space of that cleavage, fragments of commentary construe a blocked work, traces of a history whose only index is a wound without a body.

The sentences that result *ruins of documented voice* can't account for the forces pressuring their construction and decomposition, their fractures and faults; nor can they measure the entropic drift of the very discourses and archives by way of which the subject might recover its own desire, a desire memory can only betray or disavow.

Rather than foreground these facts through transparent acts of transcription and recontextualization, rather than negate the text's subjectivity by sentencing it to social fact and linguistic surface, Buzzeo's appropriations obscure their archival support, discovering language in a terrifying state of suspension between figure and ground, even while acknowledging the opacity of its own production and returning the clarity of the sentence to the performance of that obscurity.

---

infiltrated in the early- and mid 20th century by a surge of mostly second generation immigrants desiring separation from the city. In the 1980s the immigrant families who populated Long Island were the children of Levittown. Baby boomers from all over Europe. Broken languages erased and process by row houses/ Jewish Italian Armenian. The bombs were over. There were no more riots in the streets. The names had been processed changed turned over. As the asparagus farms had given way to square front yards. Shorn. The Native American town names subsumed in museums. A localness that pervaded hunger. The foreignness given to whom to what?" Buzzeo, "An Elegy" (15).

3. "The Two Books: Part One is simply called Book and is comprised of a series of testimony statements in and out of language. "Part Two Breach, Recoil is a space of commentary or the commentary of an outside made possible. In this way an inside was finally constructed and named." Buzzeo, "An Elegy" (21).

For Want and Sound arouses subjectivity in a state of ongoing expectancy and construction, longing and want, like Julia Kristeva's "subject on trial" for whom experience, narration, and body have all been cleaved *entranced* a subject constantly dissolving into its constituent parts, de-realizing the documents that make it what it is.

For Want and Sound is language aroused, collapsing in its elements.

•

Testimony can only ever bear witness to the structure that produced it *police, language, law* a hole in the story that generates no sound, and the terror of that silence. To bear witness to myself is only to perjure myself, the subject being this effect of perjury's good conscience.

Outside the testimony: your body moves as if unhindered. Inside the sentence: my body, captured sound of letter and longing. Outside the law: no sentence, no subject. Inside the body: this rent in skin and voice. Outside the longing: a blank where your body never stops coming.

•

Picture a house, an order of stories threatened with foreclosure, collapse, abandon. A subject emerges from the courtroom, the effect of a sentence. What remains outside the sentence can't be grasped. This is the shame my body bears. Make a cover. Flood the house. Go under cover. Set fire to the archive. Become subject to the cover. Make the room disappear, the sentence collapse.

It's unbearable to hear a sound that exceeds its cover in the space between letters, this endless fault, a body I will never have, abyss of endless interpellations *you you you* and the vastness of address exceeding every target, for want and sound will never coincide.

Now blow the fucking cover.

•

> *To be engulfed but to retain that loss of self*
> *in the memory of skin.*
> Robert Glück

I hear you calling my name in the trance of the stenographer's record. So I've assembled my testimony in the letters of this document before losing all correspondence inside a sentence where being and existence *noumena and nomina* will never coincide.

To cast a spell to break the spell of the court: this may be the apotropaic work *For Want and Sound* sets out to accomplish as it registers a breach in the law, a rent in the community, an illegible scar on the skin, a betrayal of the sentence. Reading this book, I'm moving in a language that wants more than any sentence can accommodate, a medium that can only fail the body in its effort to render an account, as it presses the subject into obscure submission.

This corresponds to what Buzzeo refers to as "the end of the image," where an excess of light illuminates the very place at which I fail to appear for my sentencing, a place of unremembering, the future of a body that never stops coming and the memory of that future (66).

Already decaying, what I hear is this erosion of sound, a generic failure of the sentence *everlasting feeling* to coincide with its image, just as the body fails to coincide with the self, a fantasy *thrown light* casting competing shadows on courthouse walls *court as cave* where a sentence encloses sound, forever separating subject from source.

My sentence, this place of house arrest.

•

Do you always have the same kind of feeling in relation to the sounds as the words come out of you or do you not?
Gertrude Stein

Sound. Buzzeo's book hangs on a paronym suspended in the space between incommensurable semantic values: auditory vibration and body of water. Both involve separation.

In *Tender Buttons*, Stein writes regarding sound, "A sound, a whole sound is not separation, a whole sound is in an order." A whole sound can't be heard because it can't be articulated, articulation depending on separation, forgotten ground of no law, pure extension of my body in space before being sacrificed for language.

A body of water called a sound separates one state from another, one land mass from another, one body from another.

Again, in *Tender Buttons*, Stein writes, "The kindly way to feel a separating is to have a space between." Kindly, being the affective quality of feeling difference, but also the making of "kinds" *genders and genres* thru the very act of separating. Separating gives way to wanting. In separating, the I becomes a fault between body and voice, falling into vast address. *For Want and Sound* performs a structure for this kind of feeling.

Whatever sound resists falling into separation maintains its continuity with another order, a source that can't be spoken *blank where yr body never stops coming* an order that exceeds both written law and sentence, an order beyond archive and document, an order beyond truth.

To fall out of that other order, to fall into truth: this being the meaning of disaster.

•

The ground will give way. The court will collapse.
Melissa Buzzeo

What does it mean to receive a sign from the future? What is the future if not an other order whose sound is discontinuous with this sentence, this image, this body? Clairvoyance. Prophecy. To hear a sound coming from outside this episteme, this order, this law. Life of the fugitive sign with which all correspondence will have been broken at the point of departure.

For Want and Sound concentrates just such an excess of significance, whose crisis is the impossibility of communicating the force that produced it: blocked memory of continuous sound and endless skin. This writing channels a clairvoyance, a longing to hear something outside the testimony within which a subject finds itself sentenced. To follow the fugitive sign of prophecy *against the rule of law* wherein all communication breaks along a fault that might otherwise found our fragile communion.

The testimony sings a hole in the world, a void or entrance where my body goes on longing for yours, falling thru an opening of rooms, stories, sounds, countries whose names fail to coincide with anything at all.

A sentence that never finds its period is not a sentence. This is where love begins, in a sound that wants *fails* to fill the vacancy of this everlasting feeling.

Ypsilanti, MI
September 2012

Borrowed, Mentioned or Invoked:

Butler, Judith. "Violence, Mourning, Politics," in Precarious Life: *The Powers of Mourning and Violence*. London: Verso, 2004.

Buzzeo, Melissa. *Face*. Toronto: Book Thug, 2009.

— . "An Elegy for Passage: For Want and Sound," in *TrenchArt : Surplus (Aesthetics)*. Los Angeles: Les Figues Press, 2012.

Glück, Robert. *Margery Kempe*. New York : High Risk Books, 1994.

Kristeva, Julia. *Revolution in Poetic Language*. Trans. Margaret Waller. New York: Columbia University Press, 1984.

Stein, Gertrude. "Poetry and Grammar," in *Writing and Lectures 1909-1945*. New York: Penguin, 1971.

FOR WANT AND SOUND

Under the open sky in a countryside in which nothing remained unchanged but the clouds and beneath these clouds, in a field of force of destructive torrents and explosions, was the tiny, fragile human body.

Walter Benjamin

It is when one has been able to reach the moment of opening oneself completely to the other that the scene of the other, which is more specifically the scene of history, will be able to take place in a very vast way.

Hélène Cixous

A community of decision, of initiative, of absolute
initiality but also a threatened community in which the
question has not yet found the language it has decided
to seek, is not yet sure of its own possibility within the
community. A community of the question about the
possibility of question.

Alphonso Lingis

Text beneath text.
Bone beneath bone. Unreachable, lacking
the desire distinction—touch
Bridge beneath bridge.

The polluted waters of the story in the back.

Instead of moving we kept making additions,
imagining additions. Window terrace room.

The men never came.

He hated his neighbors and drank easily their water,
saved below text.

A baby book.
A flyleaf.
A bible.
A bottom.

The rolls and reams curled so tightly.
The effervescence, translucence buried
Bequeathed but not in time.
Her picture falling out.
The floorboard that nothing could hold.
The innocence the projection.
But it was so long ago.

The book beneath the bed.

The cover completing story.

A bridge that no one mentioned. That curled against
its own beginning. Which was marked
in stone. In curl calamity and leaf.
In rotted twining. Calm.

The word for when.
For want.
For hold, for help.
The Sound covering our speech.

The room for want and sound.
Structure and sand.

A rocky beach.

A breech birth that no one remembers.

Closer to the door or to the window.

And the roots that needed to be wrung out.

Book

I want what no language holds.

Nathalie Stephens

I

Names, leaves, jackets with stripes.

A number for a name.

Beneath the covers
was a sailboat.
What I feel pressed
close to the tree.

A number for a nation.

They couldn't believe it. Nascence
away and
into my head
a question.
Into my head a list.
I stood up and was counted.
No notion going to ash.

Act 1, Step three.

The rise and fall of the balloon.
The many balloons.
The man on the bike.
The rise and fall. And the animals (red, yellow,
purple).

That we made.

Of him.

Gasping for breath.

The noise above the static.

The nation calling to me.

She drew a rope around the bed.
Made breath, rope.

Jackets with stripes.

He touched me there and there
I touch you.

There—

She drew a rope.

At age 19, long-legged and shiny haired.

We laughed at the sprinklers,
the rain falling softly.

Next to our mother in the soft light.
This light, now this.
This position. As the film goes on and goes away.

We laughed at the rain.

He was, but not quite.

He was someone who walked stiffly from door
to door.

Booklet of shadow.
Fountain of shadow.
Form of shadow. Equation.

She was someone who lay down and was still.

We were in our house, and then we were on the
courthouse steps.

The choice you can make is the choice not to follow.

And maybe when he was drunk he would take her.
Maybe when she wore that shirt.

As the little boy bounced on my leg.

Into the air and then not in the air.

A shift, then, now.

There is no air here. My cell is so clean
you could eat off it. My air is so clean
you could breathe in it.

I am losing my hair.

As the line recedes.

Bouncing beneath the sailboat the rain.

Because we never could be watered enough.

Take a bow. Have a seat. Have the courage
to sit down.

A constellation.

She asked me in:
Don't sit on the toilet. There are roses
on the walls. We don't want to catch things.

A piano, a bed, a bath.

The film covering my seat.

Everyone else has time,
but we have hundreds.
Everyone else asleep.
But we—

If you hadn't broken it, I never would have
come.

The new research says that breastfeeding for
longer than two years is now found to be
beneficial to the emergent child.
He or she receives nutrients,
is protected from disease.
Cries less, speaks earlier.
Is protected from disease.

He was of the present, of the nation.

His step was all shadow.

———

Become:

Clown, publisher of underground zines, fiction
writer.

Memoirist, become.

They stood at the doorway:

Look at my answer: genitals.

Look at my answer: ending.

In blue light, read.

He stood at the courthouse steps.

Laughing and clowning.

They were good babies, sucking on my
questions.

Latching right on. Not being afraid.

There is a white light at the top of your head.

The absence of remorse, the presence of pleasure.

Hands, memory, breath, bone.

Feeling and tenderness.

The purpose of pleasure is to rid the act of itself.

He was a monstrous baby.

To ride the act into act.

A marvelous baby.

Text into text. Act into act.

So much sorrow attached to the one book.

We said these lines in bed:
Irrevocable.
Unattainable.
We carried these lines to our country but not
incorporeal not in culture.

Is it safe in this passageway?

Expansion: I open my arms today parallel
to the sky. I am alone in this syllable.
And it is inflamed.

———

I left him finally.

My memory of the future. It's in the text.

Even on the occasion of suicide,
the beneficiaries will collect your life insurance.

Since March. It's been falling.

Because you left the line.

The risk: that you will love your baby more than
your future.

It's been found.

As we waited.

As we followed him to the courthouse steps.

On the occasion of finality.

And we were so beautiful in the doorway.

Between dissolve and image.

A penis. After all this time—

The boy in blue and the fighting beneath breath.

For blue.

My memory of it makes sense in the text.

Imagine it moving down your body.

Caressing your skull. Your throat, the area
behind your eyes, your organs.

They came into our house and shifted the story.

What I say now is the truth. They didn't do it.

What I said then was wrong.

But it was so long ago.

I take your space in my hands.

I didn't commit perjury.

A definite freedom at the periphery.

There is this definite: This dying into

That.

A body doubling back on itself, freeing itself
from all outside forces, focus, jail.

Prisoners of the second half.

A body that waits, that sprinkles.

Everyone wants to construct their story in a
doorway. Under the doorway, inside, encased.
—the flesh feel of wood—but it is too tight there.

From birth to birth this message.

From near birth to near birth.

We skip the sentence.

―――――

But an image is not a memory—doorway?

Her light hair, her weight.

Beneath the frost fronts, the marriage bed, macadam.

A basement, a bed.

Beneath the underground rage.

Paper.

Against all unit.

He taught me the piano, music, a system in a box.

―――――

I lost all correspondence with the image.

As the two sheets come together.

The content absorptive.

And tried below water.

Become: Linguist.

And is there music outside of room.

A room outside of language.

We matched our voices to theirs.

He watched me fold.

Across this line.

Inside and outside this one address.

A reach outside of sentence?

I want a separation of letters.
All this white on the floor,
this gold.

As root pushes past root.
As the nothing holds.
Releases, holds.
A baseness, a bareness pushing through.

What a name can allow.

What a name can drop off and leave.

I stepped into the vast address.

The vanished village.

Deep and parched.

Row after row.

Text after text.

Not the beyond, the before.

There is a train that runs through our town.

II

―――――

Charge the light the stare, take the picture.

In accordance.

In accordion

His blue eyes.
Laughing.
Clowning.

My magic. That appeared on the steps.

This is not—where all those lines are crossed.

In message,

In macadam.

But there is no air in this part of the train.

We followed him.

To the courthouse steps.

Because between the sun and the earth.

To pursue music.

Patterned pressure. Near the top, tip. Of the state.

To prepare: music.

Patterned silence.

Act.

I dissolve the right.

This message.

Arranging the light, the chairs.

I dissolve the right.

As we charted: subject.

As we charted: soon.

Slipping through the sills, the macadam.

The sheet that becomes a floor that
becomes a memory.

That becomes a floor.

It floods here.

Often.

As you arrange yourself in space.

In stilted silence.

The entrance. Of entrance.

There were many turns.
He was beautiful.
His hair in his pockets.

In measured macadam.

Toward the piece.

The partition.
In my part.

Counting backwards, the shapes.

Combing backwards.

Led, lent. Tilted to one side.

Measure this moment.

Lead.

And motion aside.

Evolve. Toward the window.

How high is the sprinkler supposed to go?

And if you prefer instead of light: Vapor.

From right to left.

From left to right.

She remembered: the sheets hung out to dry.
Afterwards when all the sprinklers were still.

In shallow swallow.

It came to an end.

Up and down, the base of you

The bottom of you.

Apparent.

Stoppage: a rest.

Apparent.

This house opens up to the sky (house)
in perfect syllable.

In motioned measure, semblance.
In mentioned measure.

Folding toward the story.

I lost all correspondence with the image.

Also at some length.

The voices here are very quiet.

The voices here are painful in their simplicity.

Partial in their air.

A visual chord.

A line—from here to the story window.

It was very soon, afterwards.
That we came.
To the end.

———

In experiencing the break
In according
The break
In measuring the break
Against
Itself.

It was very soon. Afterwards.

Now when all the voices are stilled.

It is very hard here: future.

In the dark. By the leaves.

And you will be:
a teacher, a doctor, an activist lawyer.

Through the marriage bed.

Come.
And when.

There is water that is coming right at me.

And when I am 18. When I am 6. When I am 12.
And 22.

Face to face, act to act.

The pressure to be is the pressure not to be.
He cried for the people inside. And laughed
on the courthouse steps.
I was trying to mark time.
1949

1972
1977, 1980. My baby on my bed—

Floating into moment.

I kissed her through the story.

Fine blue eyes, shiny dark hair. A nose.

As the two sheets come together.

We sang through the story.

I kissed her through the story.

————

The beginning that still exists, no longer readable.

Because we could never be watered enough.

Wanting to turn the pages.

Overturn the pages.

In prison where I no longer existed.

Every song imaginable.

How can I move out of the other book?

———

Because Ophioussa becomes Portus Cale,
Portus Cale becomes Portugal.

New Amsterdam New York.

There is Liberia.

Pannonia becomes Hungary, Gaul
the French Republic.

Next to our mother in the soft light.
This light, now this.
This position. As the film goes on and goes
away.

To draw a line.

And Germany is split suddenly into east and west.

———

And what is radiant becomes dissolved.

The dust outside the distance inside.

But I turned the pages. Too quickly.

———

I have never forgotten.

In the acquiring of: This.

Wanting to mistake the pages for
the turning of the pages.

———

Feel your arms, the beginning of your body,
your breath beneath you.

Let the voices erase themselves.

And into the text every day, new ideas
that have no place.

I lost all correspondence with the image.

He's my husband, he doesn't belong to you.
He's my father, he doesn't belong to you.

Trying to align the middle of that book with the
beginning of this.

The vanquished village.

Twenty-six: I am her child.

———

What cannot be exchanged.

The most lucid, the most clairvoyant.

I want in this letter: A corridor.

A vestibule standing culture.

A book like a glass eye.

When one country becomes another.

———

He entered one room. And then another.

Feel your arms, the beginning of your body,
your bed beneath you.

One form and then another.

And what does story have to do with the end of story.

The courthouse steps were about exclusion.

Trying to align the middle of this book
with the beginning of that.

What I desired most was ceiling.

———

A peninsula culture, a green light waiting to appear.

And the numbers that meant person. Or probably
in a chain like that: Nonperson.

Let the voices erase themselves.

Allow the sentence.

Sky.

———

What is radiant.
What is dissolved.

What is read to me.

———

Outside of house, the blue lines.

The smudge that stood for street.

What gets lost in document.

St. Petersburg becomes Petrograd.

Becomes Leningrad.

Becomes St. Petersburg.

We huddled together. By the yellow.
Against the sound.

There is a white light at the top of your head.

A picture part of translatable.

Past Europe. Part of Europe.

As we watch the man walk down the street.

As object of our own dissolve. The nothing—
held away.

––––––––

A body tilted until it is almost a wall. And then
still more wall.

We huddled together. Against the street.

A house.

As all notes follow another.

I unearth this step from time.

––––––––

A moving past body and back into speech.
We all got back into the same bed.

———

Choose stairs that are beautiful to you.
Your feet are on the first step.

Put your hand on the railing.

And the film?

A country that becomes itself.
A century that undoes itself.

In defense, shivering like that.

We cross the street.

———

She came, undressed in sound.

They pulled out their papers.

Their participles of sound.

———

Because Majorit becomes Madrid, Lutetia, Paris
and Alis Ubbo, Lisbon.

Athens stays as it was?

Montauk, Amagansett, Setauket, Quogue.

Because beyond the doorway.

And Berlin was once the capital of Prussia.

The Polish town of Łódź.

We drew a map.

———

There are letters that are coming right at me.

What this meaning would address.

I opened my mouth, I rushed toward story.

As you are incomparable.

Your bones are radiant inside this water. I will put it in the book.

Dancing in the destructed corridor. Only imagined. The substantiated street. Abandoned.

Dark rooms and light rooms.

Twelve languages. And memory.

———

There is this whole which figures into speech.

III

—————

We tried to remember: Book to story, story to book.

A piece of land that promises other lands.
That gives participles of other lands.

It is very hard here: Story.

What a sentence would allow.

What a sentence would drop off and leave.

—————

I raised my hands.

Let the outside sounds bring you further inside.
Listen to my breath. Breathe—

As one would take another.

In broken sentiment sediment. One voice after
another.

Beside the window. Before the door.

As every question becomes dismantled
in our mouths.

———————

It can't be talked to, held to. It can't be addressed.

When I entered the door you had become
dismembered. As body. Still there was the slide
in story the space beneath your hands the board.

The beach. A blankness. The sound falling softly.

To be unable to spell.

———————

It could be said: I went to the end of the image.

In your sleep milk becomes day, day becomes sleep.

Did you do it.

We sung linguist.

———

For all counts. I remembered the story of the
rafters the food sent under the door. The ash
that became door. And was demolished as door.

As all matches are met. And put away.

This lapse of water: A license for someone else.

I kept my books separate from hers.

With all our arms outstretched.

———

But a book is not a thing you enter?

———

All in one breath. An assonance that widens.

As one would address another.

Here: where all meanings can start.

———

If you stay I will never come, if you leave I will
never die.

As it would be possible to drown in metaphor,
they spoke so strongly—We.

A permission for someone else.

———

I repeated our names, our holding together.

As every street gets crossed and becomes another.

———

To repave question.

You have my hands.

———

Imagine the screen moving down you. Imagine
the space in your hands.

I would have to return to remember.

Any train that you want.

———

In the synagogue the church by the water the waste.

Faces without distance. Lines that get drawn in.

A life that gets distended.

———

Become: Clown.

He was very protective of my magic.

———

I dreamt you I kept you I crossed you I made you.

As all voices cross another.

She drew one breath and I another.

And the creasings that carried no names.

————

Underground, the leaflets.

We were mistaken. One for the other.

We arranged this exchange.

It is important that things be sent directly.

————

I watched the pages of paper accumulate in my hands.

A love that needn't travel.

———————

I felt it emergent.

I followed it emergent.

———————

As we arrange a beginning.
In vowels
in verbs
in leaves.

We were a family.

This is as we are followed. This is as we are
folded, forced, and freed.

You enter into an expanse. Everywhere and
nowhere at once.

———————

And what did you give me at birth, what did you
give me at sentence.

The text coming apart: Old houses and wallpaper.

A love that needn't travel.

Follow my voice. Let the outside edges drain
you the shifts enter your mouth.

I want a different kind of court.

Hear in my voice the outside sounds. Dissolving.

———

And as soon as you write it is lost, the gesture
reconstructed the gestation exhausted out of
synch with the material that is left behind.

So close, so closed and put away.

———

The blue flame, the read flame.

They made us speak another way.

———

In the absence of water; liquidation and flight.
On lined bits of paper that we used to cover our
mouth.

Flying everywhere stuck to the roof of my mouth.

The chairs that went every which way,
the hypnotic chain, the heightened letters falling
on the floor.

In the bitterness of breath turned against itself:

A stronghold—for someone else.

———

The fingerprints that are letter.

The future that is met.

A noose that is never made.

In all this nascent speech.

In the swirl of syllables: Future?

———

I wanted to speak to the book. But it disappeared
but it didn't want me but it disappeared

———

The marriage bed that became rung of tongue
for someone else.

The overwhelming feeling unstable, my letters
next to hers my motion next to theirs our names
twinning and turning: Undecided.

To try every which way but touch.

In the faraway city the dogs that were named for
music ate the paper instead of the chocolate.

And what did you give me at birth, what did you
give me at sentence.

———

From book to book we breathed together.

From near book to near book.

Beneath the covers was a sentence I have yet to offer.

The lungs that are two.

But also one.

The pure pavement.

———

In the conjoining. In houses without porch.
In the wordless repetition, soulless reparations.
In the city outside of made. Outside of met
the starving city, the city on parade.

As we gestured towards our own bodies.

Flowers on Memorial Day,

The Kabbalah.

Joining and rejoining.

Toward our own bodies.

She raised the sky with her hands. She refused
the film and accepted the nuptials upon release.

And because they kept shifting—the languages—
I couldn't study.

————

Inscribed or reascribed the stones that are taken
away. The stones that were never properly placed.

Accent on accent refusal.

A translation never seen, seamed described
as rent a translation circumscribed saturated—
fallout.

Out of my hands and onto the courthouse steps.

————

I could never get close enough.

On this paper that lacks partitions.

And the ink that is left on your hands.

From where you stood.
From where I stood.
From where we stood.

That there is nobody else.

I can speak to this time but to no other.

———

Because I could not renounce I could not continue.

———-

A novel that was concept that was continuance in someone else's hands.

Not a code but a signal, coming wrapped in sleep.

He was someone who was unable to connect
letter, woven and sound.

To be stopped to be endless.

Inside of you all the space of decay.

The one bed, pronounced blank.

———

He was a baby that was unable to digest sound.

I took you beyond the doorway the laboratory
destruction.
And onto my lap that was leaking.

After sepia.

To be a sound digestible.

———

The skin that leaks through that is undecided.

And the bodies in space the outlines in space.

I was undecided.

The most beautiful the most under pronounced

The pronounceable distance, the partition.
Faster and faster the outline dissolving into
unanswerable speech.

It was correspondence, this name now that.

A rent screen.

The flashing lights the rejoining.

A peninsula culture.

Pretending fire.

In its own backyard.

An image that departs from itself.

———

I read you in all your undisclosed chemicals,
I cannot pronounce your name.

The crease we have yet to fathom.
The fold that was forbidden.
You who have memories of the cross.
This distance now this.
We choose the letter.

The inscription and the circumference.

We linger: This vestibule on fire.

———

In your separate space of air.
In your silent space of non air.

And the doorway that is left beside letter.

———

All the pages that paled.

That peeled.

And the comparison quite incidental.

———

In the singularity of a cell breathing in and breathing out. Trying to remember.

In unremitting fusion.

I stepped out of the frame and all that was left.

———

Bodies of water that break that end.

———

The rising and the falling.

The invisible strings inscribing away.

I held them there and there I hold you.

There, you won't get caught in the circle.

It was a question not of life but of ownership, love.

———

A step away not a step toward.

It was a question of people renouncing their seats.

———

To whom does the chord belong, the light.

———

The inability and the immobility, the delicate
fluctuations, the tones on display.

I looked at him as someone who knew many
languages.

And also the sound.

And also the city.

———

I gave up my seat for yours.

Outside beyond the touching the cells
the ancient wrenching away.

All in exodus.

Not the beyond, the before.

Beneath my pillow each night the cells dividing
the kiss slipped into sound.

As we would divide and conjure ourselves.

———

The motion given the mention exhausted.

The melody lost in display.

———

When it was all numbers. From skin to skin
the time that is divided the ink leaking the
permanence the press. To be unable to say but
to have memory of speech: This is what someone
else gave me.

—————

Everyone moved here leaving the foreignness of
tongue the gardens overrunning the house.
A cloth on every table, plastic on every chair.

Everyone moved here.

—————

In the skin that the sound gave us. To bathe
in sound.

Pure puerile sound.

To make the syllables distinct.

The pauses, partitions.

The skin that was overturned.

—————

I made a baby from my body. It spoke not
like them but like me.

And if refusal is insistence. That which they
took away. To substantiate sound.

In the new shapes in the new boxes and frames.
The future meeting our skin.

And why must you defend?

The language that went with the story.

Why must I defend.

The image stored away, adjacent to sound.

As there is no pure word.

The drainage, the deposit.

But it was so long ago.

From this distant city square. No longer remembered.

Breach, Recoil

*Who can say where individuality begins and ends,
whether the living being is one or many, whether it is
the cells which associate themselves into the organism or
the organism which dissociates itself into the cells.*

Henri Bergson

It is impossible to start here. Just as it is
impossible to finish here. But so is everything
else passage, palpable, impossible.

You come into the door, threaded silver,
weighted. You wade against the door. Remnants
of every language every centrifuge every article
except this one. A loosening that is topsoil. It is
so difficult: the prying, the loosening. The silent
body, banging.
Word or cloth
Measure or motion
Dust or decay.

The filigree beyond the door the million books
betrayed threaded in line and pencil. Cells.
Beating one to the other. Cells opening. And
then closing. Dislocated, uncontested, forming.
Found.

Substantiating arrival. One or the other.

I can't go in.

On every threshold a waiting that is not being
caught. Circumvented. Returned. This in leaves.
Left off.

Inescapable decay, doubling back on itself.
The outside blooded in vines, in leaves.
The bloody entrails, remnant name. Veins.

To forget the list the composure the bloodstream
consummate.

The place sunken in image.

The place arrested. Under article of skin.

To want it there. And then there and then there.
But not here. Here where one can spill.

Too many words mean this one. A blue door, a
found door, the rain outside and the reason
inside.

In the article below my skin

Blank light

———————

The movable changeable borders you can't
bother to look up. The names set in the stone.
In the stomach of your mouth, your house.
The movable type, dislocated unmoved.
Your inability to move. To be unmoved.

The great blank.
What was once remembered.
What was once abandoned.
Absorbed.
What was once gestured: Abandonment.

What is taking place now. On this embankment.
This addendum to the story which could not take
place. Which was all gesture place. All body or
no body. We gave up the line before we took its
place.

Its wash and its water.

And the wave that passed over me. And the
wave that passed over separating me. And then
stopped. Draining the seaweed, the nets,
the verbs back. Out of tense and back into being.

In every lost notebook (what was once embankment).
In every lost telling, papers flailing, torn
abandoned. Not even the line was dry.

In every return.
In every future return. A flinging. A twisting aside.

The rain absolute.
And the littoral doorway. The washes.
The colors. The saturations. The mix-up of words and
then retreat. The doorway that came through.

We gave up the book. We took its place.

The letter I received in the mail. The French
philosopher, the words more beautiful because
of the wash, the water. The blurring. Corridor.

Apart on the table.

I left a part of my body in every book in partial
pages, presence. Dissolved.

Dissolved
Numbness
Numbers
Decay
but for the clearedness
but for the clarity
the return.

What was left below skin. Skin that I would not
take off.
That you. That I. Skin. Apart in your
hands: A beginning.

To stand here.
And then there.
And then here.
A further here. A partial here. Heavier than left.

To elegize passage.
Before it is begun.
When the joining of the two illegible.

When you are swaddled and swathed and
surpassed by image. The falling image.
The melting image. The image meeting itself.
The meeting instead of itself.
The mouth off the chest off a cavernous passage
off, off.

I don't want to write this again. The unwriting
the writing the when of your mouth. I don't want
to be here writing. This is not it at all. To elegize
passage.

———————————

We sat on the steps in the park.
In the existence of park, way past skin.
In the middle of the calming, the nation.
Way past existence, so gestural. Your mouth
and then my mouth.
Swaddled in entry.
We read the beginning and then the end.
I was alone and then not.
The spine drawn down the middle of the leaves.
Existent, executed.
The possibility of extinguishing. We left it alone.

The leaf that needed to be filled in.
A figure.
A future.
Alone.
Towards a leaf of elegy. We sat in the park.
Swarming leaf and title, recumbent.

Read
Find
Underline
Discard

The earth bloody.
The between bloody.
And the bed clean, the discarded dusted in red.
The return that is away from me. And from here.
Facing, here. Unread.

To come back to your body and to the future of
your body.

Between the capacity for absorption
and the sound absorptive.
Between the motion and the measure.

And the two books wavering. Inconsistent,
inconsequential I reach for the most important
thing. Which breaks off.

As our two skins touch in the imperfect.

The square that is analogous to cell.
The beating back betrayal.

_____

Every notebook from time one to time two
found and flung into the river. This book of
notation. This shock and surfeit.
The ink bleeding and the mouth bleeding.
The cells sharp and cornered. Corporeal. Tinged
with water. Plunged, plummet, penetrating.
The long drown out silver that is not being met.

In disparate sheets, cells. Shells. Bound from here.

In found footage.

The surface becomes the sound
The water edging and near. Floating away.

I remember the carcass in the center of my room,
colonial. A bed a frame. Untouchable wood.
Untreatable wood, already.

Written in every corridor and then forgotten.

Remnants of every language. In this leftover sound.

It was a house without corners.
A centrality that opened up: Room.
That gestured toward the end and to its
own beginning.
The rooted leaves, the names in the tree trunk
supports scribbled over.

Written from India, from France, Quebec, Italy,
Israel, Palestine, Rwanda. In past present spoken
over. Anywhere but here. Every threshold
swung wide. The writing, rewritten sungwide,
bloodied end. Germany, retraced. And the leaves
that followed.

The pockets of sound and enclosure.

A rhythm outside of rhythm.
Outside of fusion.
The dead tree and the split tree and
the overdrawn path of left. The leaves outside.

I wrote partition to be able to erase.
To be elsewhere, partition.
Elaborate pattern, elsewhere.

What is the remainder outside this sound.

———————

So much love that it is not about love.

We sat in the park, scribbled over.

I dreamt existence of park. It was in writing.

A long bed
A sound
A vowel
A held

A held out
Avowal

You trace your pencil in pencil. You remember
the fire you came from. The before fire, burning.

The stenciled lines of the house. Stolen in weight.

A book that did not come from the body because
it was already body.

And the whole called passage, entrapment
endearment a boy's name.
A name that could be nomenclature.
A girl's but for the addition of another letter.
A boy's name that came from other names.

As our two books touch in the imperfect.

We stop here.

Stenciled in, pencil.

Eternal
Liminal
Entwined
Literal

The book binding itself, its stuccoed sentences.

Have I a right to these pages?

You back against the door. A door that has
no shield because it is shield, held. Banging.
Releasing. The cursor withheld. You give up
so much face force and are surprised to feel nothing.
Splinters forgotten paint echoes. Nothing.
The underside of nothing, the understood.
All beneath your skin. Later you are back against
the door. The systemic door, the singular, the
private the privatized. Back, the center stage.
Towards nothing. You are caught in your mouth
of beginning.

The nothing:
Evacuated
Evaporating
Extending

It is here in this particle theory that you
lie down hungry.

In the absence of door.

You lie down hungry.

The asphyxiated pattern made particular.

───────────

As our two cells meet in the imperfect. Our skin
distancing our cells. When I am being
made vessel. Touched by vessel.

The multiple the meeting the future indistinct.
Cancer, a cell that gets written down.
That resumes its own speech.
Inside and outside of body multiple.

And the one jail cell.

The one and the multiple freedom inside
of presence inside of stricture inside: Dissolve.

I am loosing my body. The skin touching
the limit of being. Placed at the limit of being:
Inscription.

That the book would be a door, a way out
a threshold.
In the story, recoil I write inside of breath.
But the want of this stricture is out.

———————

A peninsula culture surrounded by water.
The when of water.
The how of water.
The overwriting and the beneath silence:
Slippage.
The city and the juncture of the city undesirable.
The walk the car the train the walk hidden in the
juncture of speech: The undesirable.

It was just image love. You can't leave it
you can't become it. Silence on all the walls of
the city. A culture that could not incorporate
wall.

The book the wound the inscription stone.
The one place held.
To give place such a different thing.
The artificial light inscription.
To give place: I remember the walls and the
aporia remembering wall. Limit meaning. At the
juncture of city and breathe. Season and size.

And the bigger it became the less and less
speech mattered. His speech was all shadow.

More than me and less than my love for it.

A text held in air.

And its absence fusion

The image bigger than air. I can't reach near enough.

Bigger than its own body, this image love.

Flooded to an opening light. To give place
towards inscription.

The one book held shut.

——————————

The repetition of every other book.
The rejection of every other book.
The becoming of this one.
Into the air and then not in the air.
A cell that gets written down.
Pursued: A cell that frees inscription.

Because it was a peninsula surrounded by not
real water, water being the desire to say,
there were none of the words that go with water.

The other books gave me body. This one book
takes it away. As there are no more other books.
As they are uncovered and free. Uncrypted and
satiated.

Floating

Returnable
Free

———————

The image at the end of the dream:
Unsurpassable. Unpresumable moment of passage.
Surrounded by water inscription. A crescendo that
stops that lingers the limited here.

This flooded here.

The outside blooded in leaves of return.

Pursued: The music bleeding though the other
body.

The blanket part of inscription.

Already passed over.

In water avowel.

———————

It became a book without edges.

A book without escape.

Remembrance attachment inseparable.

Without escape.

There is the rhythm of return.
There is also no longer.

You address the door.
You witness the archive.
Straining past door.
Straining past swollen.

The nothing you name that you come back to.

———————

You bang against the door. You dislocate
the cell that falls. But not against the door.
Memory of cell water. The widening evaporant,
the apparition.

The one cell or the many. Both water damage.
Straining soaked.

The prison the loss to be air. The loss the limit
the cell. The tranquilized air and the body
lingual. Burning against that, the nothing
to be named.

The multiple, metastasis. Over flooding over
following reaching its own cavity of air. Its own
capacity for air. You bang against the door.
Both sides of word door crushed falling.

A compendium of lack.

And paint.

Cells: A body that widens?

From cell to cell this configuration that falls apart.

Remnants of every language. In this leftover tree.

———————

The writing that is not writing.
The waiting that is not widening.
Or wading.

On this side of paper.
Below inscription.
Beyond absorption.

Paper. A body that widens without regret.

———————————

You bang against the door. You are someone
else against this door. Inside of yourself.
And the other bodies gesturing window.

The incest we held on our tongues. The mingling
the archival the specific system of met.

I can go no further than this kiss.

This begun in body.

This insistence inscription. This accompaniment
to language. And the promise inside and outside:
Of flooding.

A future that distances, met.

On brown paper bags searched for ingested, the
other animals.
In notebooks separated from the midday sun and
torn beginnings.
On articles of clothing and other bits of paper
I swallow them back.

In books returned.
Next to other script.
Because of other type.
The safety of borrow. The blank covers.

History
Community
Geography

Poetry
Fiction
Space

Collective

Written in order to disolve to scatter to last.

In somebody else's system of open and close.
To limit. The searchable met.

Inside and outside of testimony. I separate it, back.

The contested origins that can never be found.
A rocky beach. A body of water separating one
state from another. The bridge that was refused.
By all.

In the image linguistic.
The sound secluded in sound.
And the water beside.
That did not support the corpse pose, the crawl
stroke, the singular desire, further.

In the absence of salt.
In the space the survival of stone.
A body that gets written down.

This feeling surpassing surplanting:

An empty and incomprehensible book. Your
body. Wading. Door.

That it is more than me and less than my love
for it. In the other body in the other prison
in the parks both private and public.
The existence exhausted and executed.

I wrote you there and there you wrote me: There.

The cellular door, more body than words.

More presence than pressure.

This, aside.

In the failure to catalogue.
Document flight.
House flight, letter.
I want a different kind of court. Already
so seduced more language-body than words.
In the voice of a foreigner in the voice of heat
of measure in any voice at all, cataloguing
distance. The impression that outlasted the archive.

Of flight
Of figure
Of book renounced

The empty archive surpassing flight.

Notes

Aspects of this book were written in response to the ritual abuse cases of the 1980's, documented later in such books as *Satan's Silence* by Debbie Nathan and *No Crueler Tyrannies: Accusation, False Witness and Other Terrors Of Our Times* by Dorothy Rabinowitz. These cases were tried in courts located mainly in the American suburbs.

The Sound: The body of water (1,377 square miles) surrounds Long Island and separates New York from Connecticut and Rhode Island. This penninsula culture was formed by a glacial moraine. Once heavily populated by native Americans, Long Island was colonized by the Dutch and then by the British. In the early and mid-20th century, a surge of mostly second generation immigrants desiring separation from the city arrived on Long Island.

ACKNOWLEDGEMENTS

Thank you to Ofer Eliaz, to Renee Gladman, to Bhanu Kapil, to Nathalie Stephens. Each contribution a separate unwritten, unwritable book and the sudden turning of many pages.

And to my grandparents: Catalina and Pedro, Concetta and Luciano.

Thank you also to Arianna Bennett, Rob Halpern, Adina and Andrew Levitt and The Classical Yoga Center, Juliana Spahr, Cole Swensen and my students in the testimony writing classes at the University Of Iowa.

Thank you as well to the editors of *Mandorla* for publishing much of Part Two, to Lina Oh for such generous scholarship pre publication and to Teresa Carmody, Vanessa Place and the special production team at Les Figues.

Melissa Buzzeo is the author of *For Want and Sound*, *Face*, and *What Began Us*. She has taught at the University of Iowa, Brown University, and in the Naropa University summer writing program. Currently, she teaches both Creative Writing and Architecture at Pratt Institute in Brooklyn.

Rob Halpern is the author of several books of poetry including *Rumored Place, Disaster Suites*, and most recently *Music for Porn*. Together with Taylor Brady he's also the co-author of *Snow Sensitive Skin*. He lives in San Francisco and Ypsilanti, Michigan.

Klaus Killisch studied painting at the Art Academy in East-Berlin from 1981-1986. His work has been represented in many exhibitions including the Biennale in Venice, Sezon Museum of Art in Tokyo, Folkwang Museum in Essen, New National Gallery in Berlin, Museum of Contemporary Art Frankfurt / Oder. Killisch lives in Berlin. <http://www.magnetberg.de>

TRENCHART : SURPLUS SERIES

Post Office Box 7736
Los Angeles, CA 90007
www.lesfigues.com